TABLE OF CONTENTS

Foreword

Six brave (politicized prisoner), warriors, freedom fighters, and decent men of consciousness had enough of being violated by State Correctional Officials. They decided to sacrifice their lives in solitary confinement inside one of Pennsylvania Department of Corrections at State Correctional Institution Dallas. These six brave warriors, freedom fighters, and men of consciousness are known throughout the world as Dallas 6.

On that fateful day of April 29, 2010, the Dallas 6 had enough with human rights violations by Correctional Officials assigned to the restricted housing unit (RHU or solitary confinement at State Correctional Institution Dallas let alone against the mentally ill prisoners. The Dallas 6 arose unselfishly and peacefully and protested the [HUMAN RIGHTS VIOLATIONS]. At the same time, the Dallas 6 was criminally charged on trumped-up criminal charges and falsely prosecuted by Luzerne County Criminal Justice System.

Meanwhile, an international campaign ensued for the Dallas 6 to bring attention to human rights violations against prisoners held in solitary confinement. Furthermore, Carrington Keys aka "True Life" one of the Dallas 6 and the last standout is a national hero. For example, True Life was able to do something in history that no other prisoners in United States have ever accomplished, that is put Pennsylvania Department of Corrections operational manuals on public trial. This manual is promulgated by American Correctional Associations and approved by Pennsylvania General Assembly (i.e. Judicial Committee). Operational Manual(s) govern every facet of a prisoners life while incarerated and literally teach Correctional Officials how to bend the truth and manipulate. Operational Manuals are very sophisticated and the language is technical at best.

Finally, congratulations to Carrington Keys and his mother Shandre Delaney for exposing injustice in the Pennsylvania Department of Corrections.

In Struggle. In solidarity.

Jerome 'Hoagie' Coffey

Chapter 1
THE NEW MIDDLE PASSAGE AND THE WAR FOR POSSESSION OF THE BLACK BODY

"Resent the people trying to entrap your body and it can be destroyed. Turn into a dark stairwell and your body can be destroyed. The destroyers will rarely be held accountable. Mostly they will receive pensions. And destruction is merely the superlative form of a dominion whose prerogatives include friskings, detainings, beatings, and humiliations. All of this is common to black people. And all of this is old for black people. No one is held responsible." Ta-Nehisi Coates- Between the World and Me.

From the plantations of colonial America to the modern America to the modern day slaver's correction institutions there is one theme that remains constant. To have possession of the Black body and spirit equals economic prosperity and financial security. After 500 years of slavery, Jim Crow, segregation, Black Codes and Apartheid type of domestic and foreign policies, European merchants have thrived off of possessing the Black body and spirit.

Let us not forget that we live in a country where our former slave owner Presidents like George Washington traded slaves on the stock market for whiskey. We live in a country where land was taken by theft and murder of our Native American brothers and sisters. Last but not least we live in a country that was built off of and continues to flourish from the possession of the black body and spirit.

The New Middle Passage is the prison Industrial Complex. The slave masters have developed an internal Middle Passage within the United States. The slave auctions use to be next to the courthouse and inside the courthouses of America. The judicial system is the modern slave auction. The courthouse is where they do the bidding. They use to transport Africans on slave ships that were tightly compacted with chains and shackles. The slave master would have his rifle just in case any of the Negroes made move for freedom. The penalty was death. Very little has changed.

A Black woman in Texas by the name of Sandra Bland was subject to arrest, tasered and hung in the police station simply because she resisted "possession of her Black body and spirit." They claim it was suicide. However the cameras were off. As a free man or woman, no person has the right to possess you. However, because white imperialism, white supremacy and privilege has dominated the globe for the past 500 years, this system teaches its police officers and military to act as slave patrols.

If you notice police officers and, prison guards wear the same flag on their uniforms that is worn by the military and it is not the American flag of peace. Instead it is the gold fringed maritime banner of war, because American police officers are exactly what Malcom-X referred to them as, "The Occupying Army". They are the occupying army to make sure that Black and Brown people stay put in a position of a serf- peasant in the ghettoes of lower class hell. If for any reason a person of color attempts to climb the social ladder and are not approved by the 10% he or she will be subject to having their bodies captured, detained or shipped to a plantation.

In the Middle Passage, they brought Africans across the Atlantic Ocean on ships, in small spaces, shackled and handcuffed. The slave masters have upgraded their mode of transportation. The modern day captives are transported to state and federal slave cropping Industries by bus or airplane.

There is a demand for products made by American Multi-National Corporation. This demand is made possible in large portion due to the cheap labor provided by the superhuman cargo on the State and Federal plantations, who are forced to work by the slavers or subject to being psychologically whipped, denied privileges of parole and placed in solitary confinement (mental and physical torture).

Back on the plantation whenever a captive refused to work, he or she was bull-whipped, and made an example of by being chained up and lashed until blood dripped from their bodies. The modern day whip is the misconduct system and solitary confinement. The action of the slavers in placing a person in solitary confinement is to break the spirit of rebellion and to make an example for the other captives to see.

IDENTITIES ERASED AND REPLACED WITH SUBHUMAN TITLES

During the Transatlantic Slave Trade when the slaves arrived to their new destination they were taken through a process, where they were separated far away from family and deprived of any trace of their lineage. They were given subhuman titles. This process has been adopted by the New Middle Passage. During the early years of slavery, Africans were prevented from mingling with their parents or speaking their Native tongue, thus they were subject to tribal separation. The pioneers of the New Middle Passage have also adapted this practice.

Example: Upon arriving at the State and federal plantation the captive man, woman, or child is sent to an orientation camp. The orientation camp slavers are trained to tell its newly inducted slaves that you are no longer a human being, you are an inmate. In other words you are a marked article of property. The captive man and woman is given a number. The captives are given clothing and identification cards to psychologically reinforce this new identity.

This scenario is similar to the movie roots, Kunta Kinte was told that his name was no longer Kunta Kinte but that his name was Toby, when Kunta Kinte refused to accept Toby as his name he was whipped until his body and spirit could no longer take it and was forced into submission.

The New Middle Passage has a similar system in place. If you refuse to accept the title of inmate, inmate number and I.D. Card, you will be chained up in solitary confinement and psychologically whipped. In order to break up family ties and to reinforce the inmate title, the slavers will send its captives far away from home. In order to be moved back to a plantation that is closer to home the captive man or woman must be in good grace with the slave master and "work" his or her way back home.

To work your way back to a prison close to home you must first "work" (you must slave for pennies). The highest pay in most prison slave work is 42 cents an hour. If you work in the Federal Corrections Industries you may make up to a dollar per hour. But you must be a trusted slave and considered as low risk to the slave master. However, working in corrections industries jobs means that you make products for dirt cheap that are resold in inner state or outer state commerce for mega profits. Work performed in corrections industries shops is a major source of capital for the prison Profiteers of the New Middle Passage. Such cheap labor is the main reason for this New Modernized Middle Passage.

Chapter 2
THE FEAR OF UNITY

A Great man once said "our unity is more powerful than atomic bombs." I never fully internalized the depths of this statement, until, a group of us were subjected to political persecution and crucifixion at the hands of the state. On April 29th 2010 six black men including myself stood in solidarity for violations of Human rights at Dallas Prison. Each of six men engaged in a peaceful protest of covering our cell doors in an attempt to seek redress of our grievances from a series of abuse. In turn each of the six, men now known as the "Dallas 6" were charged with "riot". Of course we were only charged after exposing to the public how the Prison Industrial Complex handles prisoners who dare to speak out against oppressive conditions. Keep in mind, the fact that violence was orchestrated and initiated by Dallas Prison guards. The Dallas Prison Guards were authorized by the local and State government to capitalize from their own acts of violence though criminalizing the Dallas 6 who were the victims of their violence.

All of the above was accomplished by the local judges ratifying the so-called "Riot", charges. In reality, the only "Riot" was a unity among a group of imprisoned Black men, in other words, a group of Black men standing together for Human Rights has always been an unlawful act in the eyes of racist bureaucrats. No matter how peaceful the protest, when it comes to a group of Blacks, it has always been considered a threat to the establishment. The Harrisburg Supreme Court even upheld the bogus "Riot" charges for obvious reasons. It was said long ago in Dred Scott v. Sanford case that a Black (slave) has no rights that 'his master is bound to respect". Keep in mind that Luzerne county Pennsylvania is the same place where" Judges were indicted for selling "Kids for Cash". Luzerne County has a long history of corruption within its local government.

The state prison system and other interested shareholders/slave-holders have a problem with 6 black men demanding to be treated like human beings so they call it a "Riot". Any form of "Black Unity" is viewed as a "Riot" by racist imperialist forces. The Supreme Court of Pennsylvania obviously believes that prisoners don't have any rights which the Prison administration is bound to respect. Any form of protest is perceived as a serious criminal felony. This is called "slavery by another name and open warfare upon basic human rights.

The act of charging prisoners with "Riot" for covering a cell door is evidence of the New Jim Crow. In the fifties and sixties when Blacks demanded to be treated like Human Beings, they were sprayed with firehoses and attacked by Police dogs. In 2010 when six Black men covered our cell doors, the New Jim Crow summoned a Riot Squad and pepper sprayed, electro-shocked and bloodily beat us. This happens not because there is an actual "Riot", but because of the fear of "Black unity". Unity among any oppressed people no matter the color is perceived by those who oppress us as a threat. In America, the prison system is predominately populated by Blacks. However most of the prisons are located in Rural White America.

The State is Sending out the message that it will never accept a group of blacks, especially prisoners united for any form of protest against the New Jim Crow. Back on the plantation, whenever slaves defied the slave-master in any ways the slaves were whipped until their backs were bloody. There now exists a similar system where mostly whites benefit. Not only are the prisons built in predominantly white areas, but the prisons are located in areas that have diminishing economies and a scarcity of jobs. A prison system filled with disenfranchised Blacks is the answer to white Americas' economic problem. With all this being said, what is the solution? The solution is Unity.

UNITY in all forms; economic, social, political, militarily, both nationally and internationally.

For a more information and an in depth look into solitary confinement and the Dallas 6 visit:
hrcoalition.org or scidallas6.blogspot.com

Chapter 3
THE FAIRNESS AND INTEGRITY OF THE JUSTICE SYSTEM

In school we were all taught about the justice system that we have. Every day in school the children pledge allegiance to one nation under God having justice and liberty for all. When I was in High school I refused to pledge allegiance to the flag. The teachers would tell me to stand and have respect for what our flag represents. I like many others was told that our justice system is based upon fairness and integrity. I have a Question: for those of our fellow Americans who still believe that the justice system is fair. How can a justice system that is represented by a symbol of a blind lady with scales in one hand and a sword in the other be a fair justice system? Better yet how can a system that is represented by a blind lady holding imbalanced scales be a fair system?

The statute of this blind lady of justice stands in front of the United States Supreme Court. The lady of Justice/Injustice is the true depiction of America's so-called justice system. The blind-folded is a true depiction of the mental state of America's so-called justice system. The blind-folded lady represents the American people who act as jurors in the justice system. Why? Because the average American is blind to the corruption of Judges, District Attorneys and Police officers. The underfunded public schools help to keep American children ignorant and blind to the truth about their government. Television helps to further perpetuate the myth that the U.S. government are the good guys, saviors and anyone who is opposed to Imperialism is the bad guy. One of the definitions of justice is to treat fairly and properly. Justice is a balance. However; America's values are off balance. More money is spent to fund wars and build prisons than to educate the children. While schools are closing and American soldiers are overseas dying to defend the lies created by George Bush and Dick Cheney, the average American citizen is struggling just to pay their bills. Meanwhile, the bureaucrats and bankers of corporate America live in luxury.

Carter G. Woodson-wrote a book titled; The Miseducation of The Negro" however in 2014 it is not only the American Blacks who are miseducated; the rural white and conservative Republicans are also miseducated. Therefore, we need to write a new book titled "The Miseducation of The Rural White Conservative American." The statute of the blindfolded lady represents all the blind (ignorant) men and women who blindly pledge their allegiance to the injustice system. If we are to ever to receive justice within this system, we must remove the blind-folds from the eyes of the American people. All power belongs to the people. Power comes from the truth because one statement of truth is more powerful than 1001 lies.

In the present system there is no liberty and justice for all, because the liberty bell has a crack in it. That's why the rich blood suckers of the poor always seem to slide through the cracks in the system. In their eyes its just for them and not for us. Freedom is not free it must be acquired. The constitution of the United States of America was not written with us in mind.

See Scott v. Sanford, U.S. Supreme Court 60 US 393 (1856). "It is true, every person, and every class and description of persons who were, at the time of the adoption of the Constitution, recognized as citizens in the several States became also citizens of this new political body, but none other; it was formed by them, and for them and their posterity, but for no one else.

Therefore we are responsible for developing our own freedom. How do we develop that freedom? We develop that freedom by becoming actively involved in progressive political movements, and therefore showing the powers that be that, we are holding them accountable. The Dallas 6, Human Rights Coalition, Decarcerate, CURE and many others are on the frontlines for justice. The power is in unity. When 10,000 people show up at the Governor's office in solidarity for one common cause, the powers that be recognize that there is a force to be reckoned with.

It makes me smile when I see thousands of people attending hearings on solitary confinement. Years ago the US government would not have even thought about having any hearings on solitary confinement, but because concerned citizens have been willing to make contact with Senators and State representatives, we are now making progress. Total and complete change is inevitable. This system can no longer benefit from its inherent corruption without collapsing. It's going to collapse on its face, as long as we continue to fight for what is right, and when this cruel system does collapse, may it never rise again. Only then can we have justice e and liberty for all!

Chapter 4
THEY CALL US VIOLENT JUST BECAUSE WE REFUSE TO BE SILENT

In 1992 Tupac Shakur had a song titled Violent. In the song Tupac Says "They claim that I'm violent just because I refuse to be silent." Like a true revolutionary spirit Tupac was ahead of his time. On April 29th 2010 six men now known as "The Dallas 6" took a stance against the violence, corruption and abuse at Dallas prison in Northeast Pennsylvania.

Although this stance was non-violent, the Department of Corruption resorted to using violence against the Dallas 6. After the Dallas 6 were bloodily beaten and left in chains and shackles for hours and days at a time, the members of Dallas 6 families and friends continued to expose the brutal torture of Dallas prison solitary torture chamber. Two of the mothers of the Dallas 6 went directly to the city council and got on the microphone expressing their dissent for the official brutality transpiring at Dallas prison. The Dallas 6 continued to be a voice of protest by exposing the real perpetuators of violence. Therefore the prison officials had to take the attention off of themselves and off of their own animalistic acts. They labeled us as violent by charging us with riot.

The government of the United States of America and the Internationalists, Imperialist minds who control the puppets in office, have always been the greatest advocates of violence. It is their agenda to make the people of America and the world at large believe that any form of resistance against inhumane acts of oppressive governments is an act of violence.

And that's why Jordan Davis was murdered but the jury did not find the ex-cop guilty of murder. That's why George Zimmerman killed Trayvon Martin in cold blood and was exonerated by the jury. Why? Because any form of disobedience to the slave master or the slave masters children is seen as a form of violence. They believe in their own minds how dare you defy us? How do you defend yourself against us? You have no right to protest torture. The only right that you are entitled to is a right to do as you are told and allow yourself to be exploited and abused, by those who are clothed in authority.

A badge in America to some cowardly individuals means a license to rape, plunder, murder and attack. A person of color can even be targeted for trying to enter is own home. Ask Henry Louis gates. Jordan miles was a high school kid walking down the street to his grandmother's house in Pittsburgh, Pennsylvania. Cops targeted him and beat him bloody and even tried to pull out his dreadlocks. The same coward pigs then turned around and pressed charges against Jordan Miles. However, because Jordan Miles happens to be black and despite the fact that he has no criminal record, the cops were found not guilty of using excessive force by the jury.

It was clear for anyone with eyes to see that Jordan Miles was only given criminal charges to cover the brutal acts of the racist pigs. However, the jury believed the cops were justified in assaulting Jordan Miles because allegedly he had a soda in his pocket. As long as the good old blue blooded Americans believe that it is OK for racist cops to do as they please to us, there can be no freedom, justice or equality for all citizens. That's right we have Black and Latino Judges, Senators, Black cops and a Black president, but what does that mean to a government who still believes in racial and class superiority?

What does that mean to the average person of color and poor whites who are still subject to the bigot classist system? If you are not a member of a certain family or social class, your government and fellow brain-washed citizens do not believe that you are worthy of any of the so-called constitutional protections.

Whenever we dare speak up for ourselves; whenever we dare declare our so-called constitutional rights, the bigots in power are there to remind us that we have no rights that they are bound to respect. Therefore it is evident that a war is going on. This war is not merely a war of violence but a war to awaken the American people from this deep coma of ignorance that is widespread like a disease. We have to remove the veil from the eyes of all the people who have blindly pledged allegiance to the beast-like system.

Recently a K-9 dog was stabbed to death, the young man who killed the dog is facing prison time for up to 10 years. However, when a police officer attacks a person or kills a person of color he faces no prison time, but maybe a civil suit. They can call it stand your ground and self-defense. But the same people who claim that is okay to harass us, attack us, and murder us just for walking while black or driving while black or for having their music too loud, they will call us violent if we dare to have the balls to stand against their attacks. They labeled Martin Luther King a serious threat to national security, not because he was violent but because he took a stance against the oppressive policies of the classist, racist government of America.

They call us violent but they killed Mumar Khadafi. They call us violent but they killed Kennedy. They killed Abraham Lincoln and every other man who became a threat to the psychological chains that are placed by the heads of the American people. But they call us violent just because we refuse to be silent. Howard Zinn pointed out the fact that there have always been political prisoners who were thrown in jail for opposing war but now there is a new kind of political prisoner that has appeared in America. The new political prisoner are the men and women convicted of ordinary crimes however after becoming politically awakened, such prisoner begin making connections between their personal ordeal and the social system. In turn they become a part of not individual rebellion but collective movements. The Dallas 6 are such a category of prisoner who had become concerned with an environment whose brutality demands concentration on one's own safety and the safety of others.

Howard Zinn identified George Jackson as being such a prisoner because of his ideals and influence reached the masses in a revolutionary type of way. They authorities decided to assassinate George Jackson. It was 43 years ago that the government killed George Jackson. However, this present government is still operating off of the same program and plot. They use political assassination and the media to kill our image in the minds of those who believe in their lies. All politically and socially conscious prisoners' names are kept in an intelligence file. They call us radicals, extremists and they call us violent. However, history shows that they have always been the aggressors and the first to commit violence against unarmed men and women. That has not changed. Is it extreme, radical or violent to demand to be treated like a human being?

Chapter 5
WHAT IS IT GOING TO TAKE?

They say absolute power corrupts absolutely. Time and time again I see government officials in this sweet land of liberty abusing their power and taking advantage of those whom they supposedly have pledged to protect. They say justice is blind. Well I say, if this current system is based upon blindjustice, then maybe we need justice with a vision. Justice that can see clearly because blind justice is only leading to destruction.

It's not a day that goes by that I don't see or hear about some judge, cop, and prosecutor or corrections officer oppressing someone.

I've seen firsthand at Camp Hill prison and Dallas prison, officers bring death upon prisoner by coerced suicide, starvation and medical neglect. I've seen firsthand judges conspire with prosecutors to hold men in prison on false charges. I've seen and been a victim of officer's brutal assaults while handcuffed and shackled down. I have seen and heard many stories about offices treating men and women less than human beings just because we are prisoners.

This includes ripping up our mail in front of us, sexually intrusive pat searches, intrusive strip searches, harassing prisoners family members while on visits.

Falsification of behavior reports for sport. Falsifying misconduct reports just for sport. Falsifying reasons to deny parole eligibility all with a big smile on their evil faces. How long will this go on before people get fed up enough to take action?

Do the government officials even realize that most of the people whom they wrong will be free to take action against them in the near future? So the big Question: remains. What is it going to take to bring this corruption to an end?

What language does the American government and the whole world seem to understand: just turn on the television you can see clearly the talk is money, sex and violence. There are two things this government seems to understand the most, money and violence. When American is not out fighting a war, it is bailing out bankers and talking about the economy. So how does this all fit into the equation?

What then will it take to get the message across to crooked government officials that abuse of power is wrong? Its plain and simple, they will have to lose their money (job security) or lose their physical safety and wellbeing. Nothings else will do. This is a nation that was founded with laws against treason. Treason consists of levying war against the United States, or aiding its enemies in war. There is a war being waged against the poor class (the majority, this war is instituted by a small minority of government officials who represent the interests of mega-corporations and banking conglomerates (private banking industry). There is a small aristocracy off public officials who represent the interests of lobbyists and private membership clubs, which is all against the best interest and livelihood of the poor. This 1% and their stool pigeons work against the economics, political and social interest of the poor and working class.

There exists in America a judicial system who interprets and enforces laws in a way that protects the interest of their blood sucking private organizations while wreaking havoc upon the poor. There is a correctional industry and a small class of correctional officers, judges, DA's, lawyers etc. who benefit from crime and profit; from displacing and destroying our families and communities. This privatized for profit prison industry build their own communities from the destruction of ours. Let's not even talk about victims. Because as long as someone is being victimized by crime, multinational corporations continue to be enriched by cheap prison labor and real estate investment trust involved in building the prisons. Do they ever seek to rebuild the urban areas most affect by crime? Hardly ever.

What is it going to take? Will they recognize the wrongs when their houses are burned to the ground? Will they recognize their wrongs if their cars get bombed, assets taken, bank accounts empty and identity stolen: Will it take for their property to be looted, their children murdered or wives raped in front of them? Will they recognize their wrongs when death visits their homes? Will they recognize their wrongs when someone hacks into their databases and tracks their every move? By then it will be too late.

I am afraid to tell you that it is so. I am afraid to inform you that it will take extreme measures for these crooked officials to not be the way they are. Why is this so and why must it be taken to such extremes to get the point across. Because we have twisted system of government who believe they are above the law. That whenever they commit crimes against the poor and disadvantaged, they are granted immunity by the American court system and the brain dead citizens who serve as jurors who believe all cops are heroes.

There is no such thing as checks and balances within the government. It's a joke among themselves. The corruption is widespread and justice stands afar. Why? Because these corrupt public officials answer to no one. They will not clean up their acts unless they can see that they can be touched. Just like everyone else. They will not do right unless they see and feel that there is a hammer above their heads. And I'm not talking about the hammer of the law, because the law is only a weapon when there are people willing to enforce them. The current judges that are willing to apply the law equally to all are far and few.

The declaration of independence of July 4th 1776 states in relevant parts;

"that all men are created equal that they are endowed by their creator with certain unalienable rights, that amongst these are life, liberty and the pursuit of happiness; that to secure these rights; governments are instituted among men, deriving their just powers from the consent of the governed, that whenever any form of government becomes destructive of these ends, it is the right of the people to alter or abolish it laying its foundation on such principles, and organizing its owners in such forms as to them shall seem most likely to affect their safety and happiness (furthermore)

"When a long train of abuses and usurpations, pursing invariably the same object, evinces a design to reduce them under absolute despotism it is their right, it is their duty to throw off such government, and to provide new guards for their future security."

Now I must ask the American people who are fed up with corruption in government, corruption in the court systems, corruption in the legislator's office, corruption in elections, corruption with police officers etc. When are you going to exercise your rights and duties to throw off this corrupt government?

Will we continue to allow ourselves to live under tyranny and modern day despotism? Or will we unite and institute a government based upon real justice, real equality, real democracy, real republic of by the people and for the people or will we continue to be victims of absolute demonic tyrants?

The choice is ours collectively to unite and make a difference. We are not powerless. We have access to every means of making a change. It starts with a thought, revolution in thinking and revolution in action. Malcom X said "by any means necessary." This nation was founded on bloodshed. This nation is maintained on action and bloodshed. So I am sorry to inform you that this nation will inevitably be destroyed by bloodshed and only way that change will come, there must be some bloodshed.

Recently I watched the move bait. In the movie it showed the power of the NSA tracking system. This move was filmed the same year as September 11 2001 terror attacks. The only person who was capable of putting up a fight against the NSA was a crazy computer genius. I guess anyone who would dare hack into the NSA database would have to be considered a lunatic? Don't you believe it! At any rate inside the movie bait, Jamie Fox was an ordinary citizen from the poor class was used as a bait for the NSA The bait was to catch the guy who was capable of stealing gold from international bankers.

In so many words the U.S. government does not give two flying fucks about ordinary citizens, but if you by any chance are smart enough to hack into NSA and steal gold from bankers (illuminati-Zionist-private clubs) they will do everything in their power to track you down. They will even use the poor class as bait. But when it comes to defending the interest and rights of the have not's. You can forget about UNCLE SAM doing anything to benefit us. They may throw us a few crumbs, if we allow ourselves to become their bait. We have to do for self and for each other.

All power to the people!

Chapter 6
HOW I BECAME A POLITICAL PRISONER

The United States government has always feared the idea of people of color becoming both consciously aware and active in opposing Imperialism. In free society, the United States government has counterintelligence officers. Within the prison system there are counterintelligence officers known as Intelligence Captains. Part of their job is to gather intelligence data about prisoners who are involved in any form of activism (fighting for freedom or fighting against the prison administrations abuse of human rights of incarcerated men and women).

Another less talked about function of the prison intelligence officers is to monitor and target prisoners who study, practice and teach Black Nationalist philosophy.

The worse fear, seems to be that one day these prison houses that are filled with young Black and Latino men, these brothers will wake up and decide that enough is enough. They have no problem with us being in gangs and wasting our energy on fighting each other or playing card games and sports all day long. However, when you have a small percentage of prisoners such as myself who study, practice and teach Black Nationalism as well as fight against corrupt prison officials. The prison administration has an unwritten code to stop us at all costs.

The prison administration has an unwritten code to stop us at all costs. When I came to state prison at the age of 19 my education about Black history, Black Nationalism and American Imperialism had just begun. Whenever I would receive any literature in the mail related to any type of liberationist movements, security officers would come to my cell and confiscate my literature. They would even take my composition note book to see what I was writing down. This would happen to anyone that I associated with. The prison administration never had a problem with us learning about or reading books that promote destruction of our communities. However, it was and still is a problem for Black and Brown prisoners to learn and advocate liberation of our communities and advancement of any agendas for that same Purpose.

I first became a target when I became involved in learning and sharing radical literature with other prisoners. The so called Intelligence officers would put me in solitary confinement for bogus misconduct charges. I decided that I had to study the law in order to fight back. I learned that the prison system was a sham. It still is a sham. Whenever I filed grievances the same officers whom the grievances were filed against would answer the grievances and then write misconducts against me for "Lying to an employee".

I learned the law and began to file lawsuits against the prison officials. The retaliation intensified into all out attacks, destruction of incoming and outgoing mail, physical assaults while handcuffed and shackled, food deprivation and deprivation of showers and outside yard etc. I learned about the Human Rights Coalition investigation of cruel treatment while at Dallas prison in 2009. At the time, I had served five years in solitary confinement and after six months in population I was placed back into solitary confinement. I was targeted by security officers who came in my cell and took my legal papers, and told me to stop helping other inmates with their civil cases. I was first told that I was under investigation then I was given false charges for abusive language and refusing an order. After writing the superintendent and giving him legal notice that if my legal work was not returned I would take legal action, I was then given nine more months in solitary confinement and charged with extortion and unauthorized use of mail and contraband. My writings on prison request slips were considered as contraband and unauthorized use of mail. There were several other prisoners at Dallas who were being held in solitary confinement on falsified charges.

When the Human Rights Coalition investigation started, myself and several other prisoners decided to document everything that Dallas prison guards were doing to us including medical neglect, destruction of property, using food as a form of punishment, denying access to water, yard, and exercise for days at a time, coerced suicide, assaults, and other forms of harassment against any person involved with Human Rights Coalition. Whenever we filed criminal complaints, our complaints were sent back to the prison for the guards to investigate themselves making us even bigger targets. I and other men at Dallas prison R.H.U. in 2009-2010 reached out to every branch of government. Our complaints were ignored.

In April 2010 we decided we had enough. They cut one prisoners water off for days and another was strapped down in a restraint chair for 16 to 20 hours, all day and all night. That was the breaking point. We decided that a group of us had to stage a protest to save our friends life and to get outside media attention, a group of seven or more people covered our doors and demanded to speak with outside officials to address the ongoing abuse. Immediately we were attacked with tear gas, no one wanted to hear what we had to say. That same day three of us were emergency transferred. We decided to get with the Human Rights Coalition and file criminal complaints. I filed a lawsuit against District attorney of Luzerne County for turning a blind eye to abuse and for conspiring with Dallas prison to cover up assaults on inmates. The District attorney's office and Dallas prison responded with false riot charges for 6 of us and additional assault charges on me, although we were the ones assaulted. No riot had ever occurred in the R.H.U., because we were all locked in individual cells.

After six years and a mistrial the riot charges were dismissed. However, because I sued both the District attorney and Dallas prison, they have continued to pursue bogus assault charges against me. It's now seven years later. The parole board has denied me release 4 times since then. Now I am told that I am indefinitely suspended from being considered for parole until open criminal charges are resolved. The statute of limitations for riot and assault is five years. After the first criminal information was dismissed, the statute of limitations have expired.

I am a political prisoner because I am being held in prison on false charges. There is a class of prisoners who originally came to prison for committing crimes, however after becoming politically and socially conscious are seen as threats and as anti-establishment. Because we fight hard no matter the consequences, the state has decided that is better to keep us in prison, because it is likely that people like us will be their greatest opposition in free society. Altogether I spent over 10 years in solitary confinement. The longest time I was in was for 62 months, after being released from solitary for six months, I was sent back for another 40 months. I was released in 2012 and was not officially placed in RHU again until 2016. Thanks to my Mother and supporters, I only spent a few days in RHU on false charges and was released after Attorneys called into the institution.

The fight continues. I'm scheduled for trial in March 2017. The crooked prosecutors are hell bent on trying to convict me on false charges for assault even after the statute of limitations on original bill of information expired. I will continue to fight until I win.

All power to the people.

Chapter 7
INTERVIEW WITH DALLAS 6 member Carrington Keys
By: Raven Rakia

Question: How is trial going so far?

Answer: It's been 4 years now and we have gone before several judges continuously fighting. There was supposed to be a trial like seven times now, but every time we go to court Luzerne County has a new trick. The tricks consist of everything from making our motions disappear from the records, refusing to call our witnesses and the court has even declared one of the Dallas 6 mentally incompetent in an attempt to separate us and break our unified spirit. It's an old trick, divide and conquer.

Question: Why do I think authorities decided to charge our protest as a Riot?

Answer: This was done for political reasons. First and foremost, the Dallas 6 were men involved in exposing Dallas prison to U.S. criminal investigation and public exposure. Through Human Rights Coalition, various publications and Senate hearings on Solitary confinement. Some of the thing that stand out are: it was the Dallas 6 members who exposed Dallas guard's involvement in homicides of Matthew Bullock and Bernard Carr. Furthermore it was not until we filed civil and criminal complaint against Dallas guards and District Attorney's office that they (DA and DOC) decided to strike back at us with "Riot charges. The District Attorney was named in our lawsuit, for Luzerne County practice of returning our criminal complaints to the Prison which allowed for the prison guards to investigate themselves. Which also caused the guards to strike back with retaliation in the form of violence, food poisoning, property destruction and false misbehavior reports. The District Attorney Jacqueline Musto Carroll was upset that this lawsuit was highlighted in the Wilkes-Barre Times Leader Newspaper on June 17, 2010, along with Dallas prison. Afterwards Luzerne County contacted Lt. John Martin at Dallas and appointed him to investigate my lawsuit. Lt Martin then contacted the State Police and told them to .file riot charges against us. Prior to Dallas 6 criminal complaint and my civil complaint there was no prison record of riot at SCI Dallas in April 2010. The whole incident was only labeled as a riot to cover up the officers bloody assaults on us. It goes like this, 6 prisoners and their families file complaints to State Police and district attorney about being about 'being assaulted on April 29th, 2010. One of Dallas 6 then files a lawsuit against the District Attorney's office and Dallas prison about other assaults.

The District Attorney's office is now under, pressure to do something. So they create a story that a riot happened to take attention away from the fact that all we did was cover our doors and ask to speak with the public defender's office. They made up another story that we threw feces on guards and tried to escape from the courthouse. Now after four years they, finally admit that they don't have the guards, uniforms nor any scientific laboratory reports, nor photographs, nothing but a bogus story. They have yet to produce any evidence that the Dallas 6 planned to escape from the courthouse On September 16 2010. They know that idiots believe everything that they read in in the Newspaper, so they tried to assassinate us with false propaganda to poison public opinion about the case.

Question: Why did you all decline the plea deal?

Answer: The plea deal was disrespectful. We have been fighting this case for four years and yet they offer us a plea deal for 1-2 years and x amount years of probation. Whatever time they could have gave us would have expired already. Plus we are innocent of the crimes charged against us. No man should have to do any extra year, month or day in prison, just for covering your cell door with a cloth. If anything, we should be offering them a plea to bow down and bow out gracefully or to be destroyed by the hands of God.

Question: Why were you guys protesting and why is your case important to the public and prisoners in general.

Answer: We were protesting because our lives were threatened and our fellow prisoner Isaac Sanchez was strapped in a torture chair all day and all night. WE had witnessed other prisoners, beaten tortured and murdered by prison medial neglect and coerced suicide. We each decided that that if we did not do something to get outside attention immediately it was bound to get worse.

Our trial is important because it expresses a dark side of America that the general public thinks only happens in military detainee camps.

Furthermore it is important for the public to see how racist prosecutors waste taxpayers money for personal vendettas. It's important to all prisoners because in solitary covering cell doors is one of the only effective forms of protest that prisoners have left and to make it a crime would give an already abusive system the power to further abuse and attack prisoners.

Question: Something Important I would like the interviewer to know?

Answer: Judge Lesa Gelb who currently presides over the Dallas 6 case use to be a civil attorney. The facts of our case involves incidents in which Lesa Gelb served as an Attorney. In 2009 Mathew Bullock committed suicide. Based upon my affidavits and others, Lesa Gelb and her husband Barry Dyler filed a lawsuit on behalf of Bullocks family. Basically Judge Lesa Gelb is aware that Dallas 6 members are targets for reporting guard's involvement in suicide/homicide of Matthew Bullock and for her to be a judge on our case is a conflict of interest under the judicial code of conduct.

Chapter 8
EXCERPTS FROM DALLAS SIX PRELIMINARY HEARING

Duane Peters was called and having been duly sworn testifies as follows

Questioned By Mr. Keys

Question: Mr. Peters have you filed any criminal complaints or other types of complaints in regard to your status at SCI Dallas conditions, human rights violations?
Answer: I did

Question: Have you filed anything about human rights violations with the Geneva Convention and the department of justice and the department of military?
Answer: I have filed several complaints on record right now. As a matter of fact I have a colonel of United States department of jag, who has instructed me at all these proceedings to file records with them. We have several complaints concerning violation of our human rights. We have several-I have a habeas corpus which has been frozen in this court for four years now. I have been assaulted numerous times and I filed numerous complaints with Corporal Wilson's department as well as with the Luzerne County district attorney's office and to my understanding right now I have never gotten any responses from any of them.

QUESTION: have you filed any grievances or civil actions against any of the witnesses in this case?
ANSWER: Sergeant Buck

QUESTION: okay can you detail any of the things that Sergeant Buck has done to you or that you allege that Sergeant Buck did to you since being in the RHU?
ANSWER: Since being in RHU I've lost 60 pounds in three months. I wasn't fed at all day or night. I've also had to sleep on cold floors with no mattresses in my cell. I've also had to endure no water in my cell for months at a time and no mail going out. My outgoing mail being brought to my door, ripped up in front of me and left on the floor as confetti, my personal mail to my family being given to other inmates, who were using that to you know, write all type of derogatory stuff to my family. I received poison in my food and left in the cell to bleed through my nose. Okay

throw up blood pass blood. I'm still passing blood right now and haven ben seen by medical.

QUESTION: how long have you been in the RHU?
ANSWER: I've been in RHU 5 years now.

QUESTION: And out of all the years that you've been in the RHU how long has this stuff been going on?
ANSWER: since I came into the RHU

QUESTION: so since your time in the RHU have you filed complaints about this. What type of action was taken on your complaints?
ANSWER: all of these complaints are frozen right now pending action.

QUESTION: were you ever interviewed by the state police?
ANSWER: I've never seen the state police –in a petition that was filed on my behalf by HRC, I was not called, they were told there was an administrative matter and I would not be seen. I cannot get a phone call, a legal phone call, I cannot get contact with the outside world. And my family is complaining that they're not receiving any kind of mail from me at all and I write mail every week.

QUESTION: so if any investigation was done in regard to what you're being charged with right now or any other incident about abuse, you wouldn't know about it?
ANSWER: I don't know.

QUESTION: You were never interviewed or anything.
ANSWER: I was never interviewed or anything.

CROSS EXAMINATION BY TROOPER WILSON

QUESTION: you were poisoned
ANSWER: yes, I was poisoned. Blood started coming out of the side of my eyes, my nose. I started pissing blood and every time I go to the bathroom since that incident I've been pissing blood in my stool. That's a matter of the medical records.

QUESTION: so the DOC has records that you were--

ANSWER: they have records. They have records. I just suffered rib—I have a problem with my ribs from a car accident and I was just left in a cell to basically to die. They thought I was having a heart attack. They just left me in the cell and told medical don't look at him. Sergeant Buck was on that day and there's record of it. It's filed with the department of justice as a complaint. It's filed with the state police as a complaint, it's filed with the Luzerne county district attorney's office as a complaint. And it's inserted into the prothonotary office of this court as part of a civil suit that's currently pending in this court.

QUESTION: did you say you filed a complaint. You named me by name?
ANSWER: excuse me

QUESTION: didn't you just name me during your
ANSWER: You're Corporal Christopher J. Wilson is that?

QUESTION: did you file a complaint with me?
ANSWER: yes and I also sent you a notice that I don't consent to none of these proceedings

QUESTION: you filed a complaint with me alleging a criminal incident
ANSWER: yes

QUESTION: when
ANSWER: it's on record

QUESTION: when
ANSWER: It would probably be in the last 3 months

QUESTION: do you have a copy of this?
ANSWER: yes, I do. It can be available for discovery

QUESTION: not that is pertinent to these proceedings, I just find it kind of odd considering I never--
ANSWER: I find it kind of odd you're not responding to none of my complaints and I find it kind of odd that I'm not—I hear all these investigations but I haven't met one person who actually met with you

QUESTION: what?
ANSWER: I find it kind of odd that you keep saying that your conducting all these investigations, but I haven't found one person in the inmate population who can say they met with you.

QUESTION: just for morbid curiosity what are you referring to?
ANSWER: I mean how you are doing these investigations when nobody even seen you or have any contact with you? What is your investigation being based on?

Magistrate: I think what he's referring to is they weren't interviewed for the charges.

Peter: not only the charges, criminal complaints that were filed with the state police which is being turned over to the OPR instead of the police doing their job

Magistrate: anymore cross examinations?

QUESTION: By Mr. Wilson - who is the Jag Colonel?
ANSWER: Who is the jag? Ms. Nicole swope s-w-o-p-e

QUESTION: And there's complaints filed with her?
ANSWER: there's complaint currently in default right now on the record and there filed pursuant to misprision of felony/misprision of treason. You guys are supposed to uphold the constitution of Pennsylvania and guarantee us certain rights under the Geneva Convention guarantees me as a prisoner of war.

QUESTION: Okay do you know what this is indicating?
ANSWER: Yes I've seen that

QUESTION: You've seen it?
ANSWER: exactly

QUESTION: did you cover your window on April 29th
ANSWER: when you say cover up the window what do you mean block it completely?

QUESTION: did you cover your window on April 29th

ANSWER: yes I did

QUESTION: Were you told on more than one occasion to remove it

ANSWER: Yes I was

QUESTION: Did you remove it

ANSWER: No I did not

QUESTION: Were you subsequently removed from your cell

ANSWER: Yes I was

Corporal Wilson – nothing further

Mr. Blum - just one Question: on behalf of my client or two questions perhaps

QUESTION: Did you cover your window for a purpose?

ANSWER: I covered my windows because I was being denied rights, and I was asking to see the lieutenant. When I saw the lieutenant I was trying to tell the lieutenant that we wanted to speak to the public defender's office. Everything was disregarded. As Sergeant Buck testified he didn't pay attention to what I was saying.

QUESTION: So you covered your window then for a legitimate purpose that purpose being

Corporal Wilson – objection, your honor, legitimate purpose is based on whether or not

Mr. Blum: this is a cross examination. I can lead

Mr. Peters: I covered my window because –

Mr. Wilson: Legitimate purpose would be a legal conclusion which goes specifically at the heart of the defense that they are trying to raise.

The magistrate: it would be his opinion whether it would be legitimate.

Mr. Blum: did you cover your window for what you considered to be a legitimate purpose of trying to get someone who would be fair and impartial and answer your grievances?
ANSWER: Yes

QUESTION: was it your intention at any point to commit acts of violence
ANSWER: no not at all
Mr. Blum: nothing further
Mr. Kostelaba: I have one Question: your honor

QUESTION: when you said you were trying to get in contact with, who do you by mean we.
ANSWER: when I said we, I meant that the prisoners that were being denied food, and I meant everybody in the RHU who were not involved in the case who were being tortured
QUESTION: does that include Mr. Stanley?
ANSWER: yes it does

Chapter 9
PROSTITUTION OF JUSTICE

Taxpayer's money is being wasted on bogus criminal charges. In Luzerne County where corruption is at all-time high and Judges are known for doing even evil under the Sun. Injustice is not uncommon. Everyone in the Court in Luzerne are in on the scam, the clerks, court administrators, prothonotary and even the Sheriffs. Injustice followed by more injustice at the hands of the District' Attorneys and cronies in the courthouse in this current but four year old scheme, the Judges have lent their offices to District Attorneys and the Department of Corruption to further private and personal vendettas. The Dallas 6 were charged with riot for covering our cell doors with a cloth. To sum it all up, the criminal charges only came months after the Dallas 6 and their families filed criminal and civil charges against both the prison and the District. Attorney's office. In order to add hype and a false sense of credibility to their phony "Riot charges, the Local government released a story to the press that the 6 men planned to escape from the courthouse and that guards were assaulted upon entering our cells. After filing Charges against Carrington Keys of the Dallas 6 for allegedly throwing bodily fluids on the guards, the District Attorney claimed to have DNA evidence which proved that the charges were factual. After 4 years of false allegations, the District Attorney's office now admits that no such DNA evidence exists. Was this evidence ever lost or destroyed? If a Prosecutor has DNA evidence linking a person to a crime would he want to lose this evidence? Not unless there is something to hide.

On January 21st 2014 the Dallas 6 were subjected to another injustice at the hands of Luzerne County Corruption Ring. The dishonest and dishonorable .Judge Lesa Gelb while acting as a puppet for the District Attorney's office, decided that it was ok for the Commonwealth to destroy evidence of Laboratory results and officers uniforms that were supposedly soiled with bodily fluids, Lesa Gelb decided that it mattered not whether the Prosecutor said earlier that he would provide laboratory evidence or Scientific evidence of tests performed on guards uniforms which proved that officers were hit with urine and feces in the process of coming into my cell. This evidence is now supposedly missing from the State Police evidence lockers.

In essence Judge Gelb ruled that it's ok for the Commonwealth to conceal or destroy evidence which could in fact prove my innocence. Judge Gelb engaged in prostitution of justice by allowing the Commonwealth to move forward on charges that allegedly involve DNA evidence being thrown and while allowing the Commonwealth to conceal such exonerating evidence, which proves the charges are false.

This makes. Judge Lesa Gelb is a Prostitute of Justice and the Commonwealth District Attorney's office are her Pimps. After going through a series of Judges, Judge Gelb was personally handpicked by the District Attorney's office to deprive the Dallas 6 of a fair trial and to molest us of our rights to a compulsory process for obtaining evidence and witnesses on our behalf. To add further insult to injury the Dishonest Judge Lesa Gelb went on to deny the Dallas 6 "Expert Witnesses related to the Conditions of Solitary confinement that we are protesting. In order for the Prosecution to prove its case he must show that each of the Dallas 6 assembled together for an unlawful purpose and acted to assist one another in Riotous or turbulent behavior. The conduct that would put fear in the public's mind.

In Rebuttal of the Riot charges the Dallas 6 must show evidence that we were protesting for a legitimate purpose and that the conditions and threats to our health and safety were in fact the cause of our protest. For the dishonest and dishonorable Less Gelb to deprive us of our right to call expert witnesses, to support our defenses, is a blatant violation of due process of law.

According to well established Pennsylvania case law, a defendant has a fundamental right to present evidence provided the evident is relevant and not subject to exclusion under any, established evidentiary rule. However, in Lesa Gelb's courtroom and in Luzerne County Pennsylvania, Judges make laws as they go along and whenever the law is written in favor of the defendant the Court will interpret it in favor of the prosecution. This is called Judicial Tyranny at its best. At this moment and since the beginning of this case, it has been the mission of the prosecutor and their prostitute of justice to deny the Dallas 6 to a fair opportunity to properly answer to or rebut the false charges against us. To add more insult to in injury the dishonorable Lesa Gelb refuses to make a ruling upon our motion for a change of Venue and Venire, only because she knows that we can Appeal it to the Superior Court of Pennsylvania.

Judge Lesa Gelb is also refusing to rule upon the omnibus pretrial motion for preclusion of the justification defense. Again another example of how the District Attorneys are her Puppet Masters.

One business day before trial the District Attorneys filed an omnibus pretrial motion. The rules of court require the omnibus pretrial motions are filed within 30 days of trial date unless the evidence was not known previously. However, the district attorney's office did not raise any issues that they were not aware of, prior to filing said motion to preclude justification defense. The DA does not want us to be able to raise the defense of justification or necessity because it gives every citizen the right to defend himself and his neighbors against a perceived threat. In the minds of the Dallas 6 the threats were real because we had witnessed our fellow prisoners being abused by the prison guards and were also threatened with harm. Whenever a court official allows the court to be used for a private vendetta of the government this is called prostitution of justice.

Chapter 10
LETTER TO CROOKED JUDGE LESA GELB

To: Judge Lesa Gelb
From: Carrington Keys 12-25-13

When you assumed the role of a Judge of law, you were subscribed an oath in office or affirmation to obey, support and defend the constitution of the United States of America and the state of Pennsylvania wit fidelity. Any other oath of allegiance to the contrary notwithstanding. From the stance you have taken against myself and others charged makes it quite obvious that you have no regard for the law nor the constitutional rights of the accused. It has been your agenda from the beginning to rush us to injustice. In September 2012 you violated the law by calling us to court while appeal was still pending.

It is obvious that you are a puppet for the prosecutors and as long as you are a criminal judge, you will continue to allow the district attorney's office to pull your strings. You call yourself a judge but in all actuality you don't even have your own voice. Your corruption is being made public and the masses are being informed of your evil plots to railroad us along with your partners in crime in the district attorney's office. It is your agenda to keep this fraud private and out of the public view. That's why you attempted to remove our families from the courtroom on 12-9-13.

You were made aware in October that my continued confinement at SCI Retreat denies me eligibility for parole and vocational classes at my home prison. Yet you conspired with the prosecution to detain me at retreat as a mechanism to persecute me and force me to submit to the false charges. I will never submit to your frauds. It doesn't matter how many corrupt judges the prosecutors have in league with them. The hand of the most high is upon me and your arms too short to slap box with God.

Your friends and those of your colleagues are under investigation. Your power as a judge has blinded you into believing that you are above the law. For that reason may you continue to walk down the path of lawlessness to your own demise. Please find enclosed a notice of appeal. We are aware that you have no problem lying and claiming that you did not receive it. For that reasons I will have it sent both certified and regular mail and maintain all copies of cash slips as proof in the event you attempt to claim you have not received a copy. We are not your average ignorant subjects and every attack that you may try to execute will blow up in your face.

Chapter 11
The Illusion of Equal Justice in America and What Parts Our Leaders Play In This Illusion

In America and abroad, the leaders are the ones who hold power, influence and direction over the masses of people. This includes celebrities (entertainers, rappers, singers, musicians, movie stars, politicians, etc.). In the presence of such personalities, the masses do everything from screaming, passing out. There is a saying that if you are not a part of the solution than you are part of the problem. I have a question that I think is of primary importance. Which of our leaders is worthy of praise and honor by the people?

In the wake of the national exposure of a white officer Darren Wilson shooting and killing an unarmed Black teenager. Many influential personalities have come to show their support for the family of Michael Brown and their diligent pursuit of justice. However, I must emphasize that it appears that we have not learned from history, and therefore history is repeating itself.

I salute the people of Ferguson and the people across the world that has shown solidarity and support for Michael Brown. It is obvious that people in the hoods across America are ready to fight. They're all fired up. However, proper leadership is lacking. Protest is ok and has its benefits. But protest and riots that only result in the destruction of our own establishments only helps to strength the hands of the racist imperialistic forces that were responsible for the death of Michael Brown and the death of every unarmed Black man who have been slayed by those operating under the color of law.

The leaders for the most part have displayed ultimate betrayal by not giving the protestors proper guidance when it is needed the most. When are we going to wake up from the illusion of equal justice under the law? Do we actually expect to get equal justice from a system that was founded upon the bloodshed of our ancestors? 500 years of institutional racism, and institutionalized slavery, also 500 years of lynching us outside the courtroom and inside the courtroom. On the American flag, we see 3 colors; red, white, and blue. They tell you that white represents the people (yes their people). Red represents bloodshed. Yes, the blood of the Indian and our ancestors that the white slave masters shed in order to build this country up from slave labor.

The American flag represents your death if you are Black or Brown and also if you happen not to be a stool pigeon for the powers that be. The blue color on the flag represents the ocean that they sailed the slave ships on to get us here.

The symbol of justice in America is a blind lady holding a sword in one hand and unbalanced scales in the other hand. Can anyone expect to get justice from a blind lady holding unbalanced scales? The scales are always balanced in favor of the enforcers of law because the law enforces the laws that keep imperialism in power on a global, economic and military scale. The laws are only used to keep the poor class in check and to maintain the power structure of the Aristocratic Corporate banking families of the world.

Power yields to nothing but equal power or greater power. There are two things that this nation was founded upon and maintained upon (economic power/military power). The rapper Nelly made a profound statement while in Ferguson Missouri supporting Michael Brown and the protest for justice. Nelly said: "We have to change our tactics'. That's right; we have to change how we respond to these injustices. We have to go after the corporations and other people who benefit financially and politically from this injustice as a whole. We have to go after the people who make a living off of shedding our blood and sucking our blood. We have to form our own neighborhood police forces and security forces to prevent the destruction of Black establishments.

Do we expect the same police force who murdered an unarmed Black teenager to protect our business and churches? Do we expect the same people who traded in their Klan uniforms for police uniforms to guard the safety of our community? Do we expect the same court system that said Blacks are subhuman and only 3/5ths of a man along with Jim Crow laws are ok and separate but equal to render a verdict against one of their own? Absolutely not!

The American people have all been fed the subliminal message from cartoons, movies, and one million cop shows that all cops are heroes and the unfortunate people that they go after must be the bad guys,. This lie has been bought wholesale by the average middle class American who serves on theses grand juries. The average middle class American has not had negative encounters with police. They have never witnessed people beaten, shot or killed by the cops or framed by the cops. So as far as they can see, the cops are the heroes, and if a cop kills an unarmed Black man, hey will say: "Oh well, just one less criminal to worry about!"

Corporate government in America understands this blind faith that the average American has in the system which serves the few at the expense of the many persons who fall victim. This is why they created a story that Michael Brown was a criminal. Although the story was a fabrication because no one paid attention to the fact that Michael Brown actually paid for the cigarillos that they claim he had stolen. Upon further review of the facts, not only did Michael Brown pay for the cigarettes but the video was weeks prior to the fate that Michael Brown was gunned down. In fact, the store owner never reported a robbery but someone in the store misunderstood the incident. So when the cops got hold of this tape that's when they began to work their magic and created a story that this Klan cop boy was pursing Michael Brown as a robbery suspect.

The powers that be, used their media outlets to slay the image of the Black man and to poison the minds of the masses of predominately white middle class.
The average American is blinded by false media and a false perception of law enforcement. How do our leaders betray us in this regard? Black government officials from Obama all the way down to the Blacks in the police force, instruct in the people to be calm and to seek justice in the right way, but what is the right way when we never get results from the instructions given to us by these token Negroes and four star general house niggers.

What is the right way when a war is being waged against our youth? Do we continue to listen to these intellectual slaves who make a living off of these old outdated "we shall overcome: type approaches, or do we step our game up and learn from our history what has worked in the past and still works in the present? In order to get some justice from lady Justice, first we must take the blindfold off; we have to remove the lies that are covering eyes and minds of the American people. We have to create our own systems of justice, our own police forces and our own economic security.

Your favorite celebrities made over billions of dollars this year, how much of this money was put towards the future safety and security of the Black community? Not 1 dollar. Earlier I asked the question which of our leaders should be honored or praised? Certainly not these clowns who brag about spending 100,000 dollars on an iced out chain, while contributing nothing to the empowerment and development of the community or to our future leaders (the children).

Those whom have shown their support, presence and positive leadership abilities in the community are the ones who are worthy of honor and praise. Nelly, and the St. Lunatics, Jasiri X are all noteworthy for honorable mention this regard. The St. Louis Rams players who stepped on the field with the hands up don't shoot gestures, should be honored for not having the fear of being ousted for using the NFL as a platform to express their discontent for this injustice system.

Let's call this system what it is. It's an injustice system, no wonder the Lady of Justice has unbalanced scales in her hand. If you think that you can get justice from a blind lady with a sword, than you have some serious mental issues. The blind lady is not paying attention to who she is hitting with the sword, or is she? It seems very clear that when it comes to serving justice on a White cop. Lady Justice knows not to use the sword, somehow she sees through the blindfold, but when it comes to serving justice on a Black man, Lady Justice does not need to see all the evidence. We will be found guilty as charged. Is it any wonder why they will arrest Michael Brown's dad for the comments he made after his son's death? But the same district attorney's office will not charge Officer Wilson who killed Michael Brown? The Liberty bell has a crack in it, and the crooked government officials always find a way to slip thru the cracks in this crooked system.

Liberty means freedom, so why does the liberty bell have a crack in it? What were the founding fathers and their masonic fraternity trying to tell us? They were telling us that the idea that Liberty is for all is an illusion because freedom is not free. It must be fought for. This country and the men who founded it were not granted freedom by protest they were rewarded freedom by war and bloodshed. At the time that he constitution was written there was no freedom or liberty for all, because a great number of the founding fathers were Slave owners and they did not believe in the equality of races. There has always been a class of people in this country who do not believe in the liberty and human rights of all people. This sick racist mind was passed down from generation to generation. That's why the racist bigot cops believe that they have a right to do as they damn please. They know their history and they know that White men in power in this country have always enjoyed the privilege granted to them by this government to plunder, rape and mutilate the people they deem to be their subjects and inferiors. This is why the Associated Press and other media outlets are using the statistics and other number game tricks to make it appear that the cops are only doing their job. In other words if you break the law the cops are granted the power to be your judge, jury and executioner, and the penalty is death.

Question: If it is just a job for them to kill us for the slightest gesture, than it must be our job to stop them from killing us by any means necessary. Why is it that Black people can make songs about killing each other every second of the day, but when it comes to using violence in self-defense against our 500 year racial oppressors, the gangsters have nothing to say? What happened to the Ice T Cop Killer type songs? If it's ok for them to use the media to justify assassinating the Black youth than it must be ok for us to propagate gunning police officers down as a necessary means of survival against this open and actual threat to our existence.

Violence is usually the last resort in a war that can be won overnight if we only had the unity to make these imperialists suffer economic-ally by refusing to participate in their exploitation of us through our voluntary consumerism. It's within our power to expose them and have masses of people boycott the Billionaire Corporations such as Microsoft, TWA Airline and others corporations who make fortunes off of mass incarceration process initiated by the criminalization of a generation. Like the cop who went after Michael Brown and got away with the killing him by using the stereotypical profile that Michael Brown was a criminal and deserved to be killed for this. They killed Mike Brown's image in the court of public opinion. We have a system that benefits from creating monstrous images of Black man. Therefore we must confront those who work for and benefit from this system head on by causing them to lose all their assets and stocks which they have only received by exploiting the image and likeness of Black and Brown youth. Now is the time to take action and end these injustices. Together, we can take the bull by the horns and break this beast down piece by piece!

Chapter 12
Is the Pen Mightier than the Sword?

We have all heard the saying that the pen is mightier than the sword, right?

Some things that sound good make perfect sense in a senseless word, and other things that sound good are nothing more than righteous rhetoric. It is a common teaching in the church that Jesus taught his followers to turn the other cheek. This is a teaching that has been used to make mental and physical slaves passive and non-resistant to their own oppression and to the oppression of others. It is all a part of God's plan they will tell you. Are you telling me that it was God's plan for you to be bamboozled, hoodwinked and tricked by the enemy of righteousness? That sounds to me like one HELL of a God, and not a Heavenly Father.

When anyone prays to that God they should say: "Thou Father which put me in hell", After all they said it was his plan! What is a not so common teaching in the church is that Jesus told his disciples to sell their garments and purchase swords. What was it that was so important, that Jesus would tell his disciples to sell the clothes from off of their backs and buy swords? I'll tell you what is so important, that you should put down your pen and ink cartridges and pick up a weapon, self-preservation. Self-preservation is the first law of nature. The law of the jungle is survival of the fittest. When you wake up in the morning and you're a gazelle, you're probably running from lions and other hunters. In the ghettoes of hell in North America, when we wake up in the morning, we are either running from the cops or running from the gunshots of genocidal violence.

Malcolm-X said it's either the ballot or the bullet. Do you see what we have been getting from using the ballot, nothing but a few Black faces in position to uphold White lies. We should all now be able to see that Obama was put in position to run for office only to sell false hope to future generations of children. The real message from Obama's presidency is that White America will allow you in office, but you better not have the best interest of Black people, you must pledge allegiance to the flag and cultural practices of White Supremacist Imperialism.

The question still remains; is the pen mightier than the sword? The answer to that question is complex enough to cover volumes of shelves in the Vatican's Library. During the crusades swords were used to fight a war over control of Jerusalem and what lied buried there. In our modern day crusades it is a war between truth and falsehood to conquer the minds of the masses. A certain class of Europeans are fighting for their genetic survival, in the face of the world and America itself becoming Blacker and Browner.

In 1968 the Movie: "Planet of The apes" was released during the time of intensifying race riots, My Lai Massacres and the government sanctioned assassination of Martin Luther King and Robert Kennedy. According to Life Magazine, the movie reflected the fear that the established order would be uprooted by civil unrest. Eric Green in the "Planet of the apes as American Myth" stated "there is a long standing fear among Whites in the United States of-- a loss of racial dominance."

He later went on to say that these fears were aggravated during the sixties by the war in Vietnam and the struggle for black liberation at home in America. There was a sense that racial violence was beyond control. At the end of Planet of The Apes, the statue of Liberty is buried up to its neck in the sand.

Here in 2017, with the recent election of Donald Trump, we see this same white fear and racial violence along with the black liberation struggle at the forefront with the Movement for Black Lives. Back to the question at hand, is the pen mightier than the Sword?

Yes, only if you are using it to educate and open the eyes of the masses to the opportunity to be on the right side of history. If your pen is being used to win people over in our fight for liberation from imperialism and the right to self-determination, than the pen is mightier than the sword.

However, there comes a time when you have to put down your pen or your I-Phone and pick up arms to defend yourself and your community. We don't only need a legal army of lawyers to defend us in courts, but we also need our own Black Security Vanguard to protect the people in the community from the vultures, buzzards, and parasites in the American Fraternity of Police (Blue Klux Klan). We need self-government. For as long as we are governed by enemy forces, we will continue to be subjects of arrest for profit, shoot to kill, conviction for profit, tickets and fines for profit etc... We need police forces of people who look like us and who think like us. We don't need a police force full of people who believe that every young man or boy of color is a gang member, thug or criminally insane psychopath.

We also need ex-cons turned entrepreneurs to be willing to go back into the communities and sit down with at risk youth and show them a better way to financial success and economic empowerment. Teach them to use their pens to write business plans and or job applications. If they trade in their guns for knowledge of how to write out their future and life's mission statement, that's how the pen becomes mightier than the sword.

The flip side of the coin: Crucial times call for crucial methods and desperate times call for desperate measures. When your backs up against the wall. There's no time to write only time to fight.

Chapter 13
The Livelihood of the Police State Culture Is the Demise of Black and Brown America

The Black people here in America have always been a source of revenue on the shores of the United States of America. Any talk of police accountability and criminal justice reform is frightening to the prosperous industry of policing in America.

There is a not so popular history of policing in America that is tied directly to slavery. The first police in America as we understand police in this day and time were slave patrols.

To learn more about this direct connection between slavery and policing in America one can read various Supreme Court cases which detail the laws, policies and treatment of Blacks by White authorities in both pre-civil war and post reconstruction times. See Hodges V. United States, 203 U.S. 1 (1906).

The Supreme Court states "In slave times, in the slave states, not infrequently every free Negro was required to carry with him a copy of a judicial decree or other evidence of his right to freedom or be subject to arrest. That was one of the badges and incidents of slavery."

Essential to the right to freedom is the right to travel. A Black man woman, or child cannot even walk down the street without some racist cop demanding to see license. Whether you walk, ride or drive, the White establishment is there to let you know that you can be arrested at any time and your right to travel is only a privilege that is subject to be restricted by the executive privilege of White Supremacy.

After Black Americans were freed by the 13th Amendment White America passed vagrancy laws to put Blacks back into slavery. These vagrancy laws or Black codes have been modernized by the descendants of racist White America in this modern police state. For instance, a woman in Ferguson Missouri has a domestic dispute, she calls the police on her boyfriend, the cops arrive and the boyfriend is not present. The police asks the woman if her boyfriend lives in the home. The woman answers affirmatively. The police then place the woman under arrest for not having an occupancy permit with her boyfriend's name listed on it.

Such laws are the badges and incidents of slavery because Blacks have always been the source of revenue for White establishment. Incidentally, laws are passed by White America which target Blacks for arrest, prosecution and conviction in order to fund the police state and prison industrial complex. Some misinformed individuals want to know why we have a problem with the private for profit prison industrial complex. I'll tell you why we have a problem with it. Because crime and profit go hand in hand in this current state of prison for profit politics. Black and Brown bodies are being possessed and confined along with poor Whites for the sole means of economic advantage and exploitation for rural White Americans. Places where no means of financial opportunities exists are the places where most prisons are located. As a result of their being a need to fill the cells of said prisons, Blacks and Latinos are targeted the most for arrest and conviction.

Correctional officers unions have a political, personal, and financial interest in continuous incarceration in order to ensure financial security and continuous profits. Small counties of White America are politically motivated to push for legislation which indefinitely incarcerates mostly Black and Brown prisoners.

Why? Because as long as there is a prison in rural county America, there are more people to count on the county census for tax dollars from--the U. S. government.

The same counties that receive tax dollars for counting prisoners on the county census are not willing to provide any benefit to the prisoners-who are responsible for the financial livelihood of these rural counties where most of the prisons are located. The same counties which benefit from having prisons full of Black and Brown bodies are not willing to provide jobs to felons upon their release from prison. Most of the" prison employees look down on the men, women, and children in prison. However; if it weren't for the prisons being constructed in these small farm towns of rural America most of the prison staff would not have a job.

Chapter 14
Fighters, Activists And Protesters: Where Are You?

There is an old African proverb that reads: "Unity is strength and Division is Weakness".

I have a question to ask to all of you movement members, activists, revolutionaries and human rights organizations, where are you?

A call to action was made for a peace and Justice rally for Martin Luther King and the Dallas 6. On January 15th 2016, a rally was held and it is a disappointment that not many people showed up. So I ask the important question where you were when the men in the struggle needed you.

Before it was popular to protest Police abuse, 6 men known as the Dallas 6 staged a peaceful protest in solitary confinement, and were subject to official brutality, bloody assaults and false charges for riot.

A call to action was sent to several frontline organizations, such as Black Lives Matter, Color of Change, NAACP, and others. However not one person from any of these organizations showed up to support the men who are being held in prison for false charges, our only crime in this case being black men who chose to peacefully protest abusive racist white officers.

The media showed up and we needed your support and presence there to let the government know that all Black Lives Matter including brothers and sisters who are held in prison for crimes we did not commit.

A call has been made for your support, unity is always needed to make a statement that we will not tolerate mistreatment and being counted as less than human by a racist system of injustice.

The remaining three members of the Dallas 6 have refused to plea to false charges for six years straight. We needed the highest level of leadership we could have. The highest level of leadership is you brothers and sisters at the grass roots who are on the frontlines of the struggle. Your voices and presence is more powerful than a nuclear warhead.

On January 15th, 2016 the news media was present to help expose the politically and racially motivated prosecution of a group of Black men, however the presence the movement and voices of the movement was lacking in significant numbers.

If you brothers and sisters would have been present, the lying prosecutors would probably be running for cover right now. This is a call to action to the men and women of the movements for justice, human rights and civil rights, what is needed is for you and many more people like you, to come together in numbers to support brothers and sisters behind the walls who have legitimate causes.

Any man or woman who takes a stand and is attacked by the system for making a stand should be supported. My brothers and I of the Dallas 6 put our lives on the line for Human Rights and we needed your support in order to successfully defeat a common foe. We asked that you contribute your organizing forces to support the Justice for the Dallas 6 campaign.

Too many men and women have been left to suffer and die behind the walls of the prison industrial complex because of lack of support from the larger community of the movement. United we survive to fight another day and divided we die. Black lives matter outside and inside. It's either we build or continue to be killed by the same system of imperialism and colonialism.

Let's work together to put an end to systemic oppression.

All Power to the People.

Chapter 15
Justice or Vengeance

In America, there is a constant theme being promoted daily. The theme is the "Good Guys taking out the Bad Guys" as punishment for some offense against "We the People". The Bad Guy can be anyone from a common so-called criminal to a terrorist or tyrant. Middle Eastern Islamic leaders are usually painted as tyrants who are responsible for oppressing their own countrymen. In America, the bad guy is the gun toting drug dealer who is supplying the neighborhood with dope. The media and Hollywood does a good job at making a person appear to be so vile and wicked, that when the Good Guys (Government, Cop, Military), takes the law in their own hands and terminates the so-called Bad Guy, the American people have been programmed to be happy that the so-called Bad Guy has been terminated. The media specializes in creating a thirst for blood inside the hearts and minds of the American people. This thirst for blood is further promoted by the very high level of violence in movies and video games. The hidden message that is subliminally suggested throughout the media, Hollywood and game world is that violence is "okay" as long as it's used against the profiled Bad Guys.

This said violence can be committed against any "suspect" for the common safety of the community. Supposedly this kind of behavior (police brutality) is for public safety. The reaction desired by the promoters of the "Police State" is one that reads:

"Who cares if the Police Threw a grenade bomb in your grandmother's house, grandma should not have a suspected drug dealer in the house".

It was not too long ago that the cops in Atlanta Georgia executed a no knock warrant on a family's home. The cops threw a grenade in the baby's crib and burned the little child severely. This "Tough on Crime", "Kill the Bad Guy" propaganda has allowed for the American people to be suckered by a blood thirsty government. Under the guise of public safety, War on Terrorism and War on Drugs, the county government has been transformed into a military combat force. These police powers were secured in fraud and the disarming of the American citizens is designed to prevent any form of resistance to the tyrannical maniacs who are inside of the American government.

The government and a large number of people are calling for bans and restrictions on
firearms, but guns do not kill people. The Department of Justice is calling for investigations and better training for bias and racist police officers. I'm sorry but that's a flock of shit and we all know it. Better training will not remove bias and racism form the hearts and minds of racist police officers who know that they have a license to plunder, torture and in most cases kill a person of color or poor white. No matter how much training racist cops receive, as long as they are allowed to work on a police force, they will continue to unjustifiably beat and kill less fortunate and less privileged persons.

Every time President Donald Chump gives a sermon his blind puppet supporters are yelling out "Build a Wall" and "make America Great Again". The translation of the slogans are as follows: "Let's build a wall to keep out the immigrants, the immigrants are the Brown and Black people from Central and South America. "Make America Great Again" only means they wish to make America overtly a White Supremacist Power Structure again. Let's make America Archie Bunker Whiter by all means necessary. Contrary to popular belief and stereotype, Blacks are the number one people deported out of the country. Yes it's still "if you're Black get back" but no Brown aint allowed to stick around, not no more. They want to build a literal physical wall as well as political and economic wall to keep all non-elite, non-whites out of positions of power. What they are saying in laymen's terms is: "Build an economic, social and political wall, segregation, Jim Crow, and pre-civil war America on steroids. They want to make America the land where "white is right and everyone else get the hell out of sight." That's what they mean when they say: "We're taking our country back".

The question is: Who? Who are they taking the country back from? Certainly one half-black man named Barack Obama as President does not represent the epitome of Black Empowerment. White Americans have a historical fear of losing white privilege and having to compete with the very people that they have oppressed for 500 years. This scares the shit out of racist White America (not all White people). Donald Chump made every indication that he is in support of racial discrimination and division, among other unprogressive agendas. However 70 million blind Whites, Blacks and Latino's actually voted for this clown. Some Whites will say: We are not racist just because we voted for Donald Chump. That's like saying; Hitler wasn't anti-Jew because he himself had Jewish Blood. However; if you walk with the oppressor than you are the oppressor. If you endorse white Supremacy and Bigotry than you are what you support. D.L. Hughley made a great point when he said: "You can't be a little bit pregnant, you're either pregnant or you're not". You can't be a little bit racist, you're either racist or you're not.

As Van Jones said: The vote for Trump was definitely largely motivated by White Lash, (White people lashing out against a system that they believe is tearing away white privilege. This is why there is no justice in America for the poor, oppressed and have nots, only vengeance. This is what America was founded upon, vengeance not justice. Our country was founded by Free-Masons who swear an oath of vengeance upon anyone who would violate or breach the tenets of the craft.

Chapter 16
THE DALLAS 6 TRIAL

Our trial began on April 4th 2016 the day that Rev. Dr. Martin Luther King Jr. was assassinated. Just as he engaged in many protests and was persecuted for his protests, the Dallas 6 were standing trial for protesting Injustice. Day one of trial consisted mostly of jury selection. The amazing thing about day one of trial is that we end up with five people of color on the jury panel. This was amazing because the District Attorney could have used his preemptory strikes to get rid of all of the people of color. I don't know if it was because the District Attorney wanted to appear fair or was it because he was confident that he would not be defeated by a group of prisoners.

At any rate, we had to strategize between the three Dallas 6 members that were on trial (Andre Jacobs, Duane Peters and myself). Strategy was necessary as always to obtain a victory. We were up against the state who were trying to knock our lights out. As part of strategic thinking Duane decided to allow Attorney and Professor, Michael Wiseman to represent him. This strategic power move allowed for two good things to happen (1) Duane played the background as an observer and was able to relay helpful insight to the rest of us (2) Michael Wiseman used the Professional angle to cover us whenever we missed anything, as well as technical advantage.

Ultimately we each had the opportunity to pick their witnesses apart. We refused to allow the judge and District attorney to walk all over us, we stuck together; we stuck to our guns. As a result we achieved a favorable verdict when all odds were stacked against us. Unity is strength and courage.

All power to the people!

View a portion of trial transcripts here:

http://tinyurl.com/ck-trial-transcripts

Chapter 17
THE LAST MAN STANDING---THE SECOND TRIAL: PUBLIC FACADE

After seven years of fighting and going back and forth to court between seven prisons, long bus rides and sheriffs pick-ups, it finally ended on March 13 2017. The first to go into a courtroom was also the last one. On September 16, 2010, I was the first and only one of the Dallas 6 to enter a courtroom where I was held for trial after attending a fast Kangaroo court proceeding. It was supposed to be a preliminary hearing that day. The same newspapers that slandered me in the beginning also put out fake news against me in the end. The proper legal term for what they did is Libel.

The Times Leader ran a story that I and the others Dallas 6 brothers were attempting to escape from the courthouse, therefore it was a need for 16 armed guards, helicopters, caged vans, and presence of several State Troopers in order to secure "dangerous prisoners" in so many words. It also stated that we barricaded our cells and threw feces on guards when they attempted to enter the cells. This same fake news was circulated by Citizens Voice newspaper.

Long behold the same crooked newspapers "Citizens Voice" and "Times Leader" would later make up "Alternative Facts" after the March 13, 2017 trial. On March 13, 2017 I attended a five minute bench trial and was found not guilty of riot or aggravated harassment. Instead I was found guilty of misdemeanor for disorderly conduct.

However if you leave it up to the "Fake News" pseudo-journalists of "Times Leader" and "Citizens Voice", they claim that I was convicted of slinging feces at guards. "Lie, Lie, Lie". Donald Trump has one thing right, If Times leader is the leader of the times than I can see why 70% of Luzerne County voted for Trump. The only thing that they are leaders of are leaders of the lies. They're leading people away from the truth. Citizens Voice is more like the governments voice.

The one thing that Trump has right: "Fake News" is the way of several media sources. They don't lie all the time, but they tell enough lies to erode their credibility as a reliable source of information. The stories printed by Joe Dolinsky and James Haplin of the two newspapers named above are definitely "Fake News". How can "we the people" trust in the integrity of the media, when the public is constantly being fed "Alternative Facts"? One would think with all of the spotlight on the news media from President Trump calling them "fake news" that newspapers would clean up some of their filthy practices. However the liars keep on lying just to have a good story to give their audience.

They couldn't just tell the truth and say: "Carrington Keys was not found guilty of throwing shit (aggravated harassment) allegations, because that would challenge the credibility of the District Attorney's office and the correctional officers involved.

Fake journalism appears to be the way of today. At least this much is true in Luzerne County Pennsylvania, the Kids for Cash Capital. What does Fake Journalism mean to me? Fake Journalism in my experience is representative of puppets who write articles containing untrue statements to appease their puppet masters. Fake Journalism is the death blow to free press, because whenever the government can manipulate news media personnel to present "Alternative Facts", the truth gets swept underneath the rubble of confusion.

On March 13, 2017 a power play occurred between the District Attorney's office and my standby counsel Michael Wiseman, who is a great lawyer and Law Professor. It was time for negotiation.

"We sit at the bargaining table for one reason-- the other side has something that we want" --How to Negotiate, Ronald Shapiro (2001).

During the negotiation process I was informed that if I accepted a bench trial than most likely I would not be found guilty of the charges involving throwing feces at guards and instead I would receive a misdemeanor or summary offense for disorderly conduct and given no additional time in prison for it.

I had everything to gain from this bargain or negotiation and so did the District Attorney's office. The District Attorney's office had the chance of not having their credibility totally diminished for being unsuccessful at getting any conviction against the alleged "Rioter". On the other hand what I had to gain was being free of a felony conviction, free of serving additional time in prison, and clearing my name of false allegations of causing a riot and throwing human waste on correctional officers.

This was a substantial gain for me, after being mistreated, attacked, harassed, threatened and denied parole four times at the cause of such lies. I now have the upper hand on my civil claims against the Commonwealth. I now have the record proof to protect my reputation as a "Stand up" man against slanderers and those who believe in the Fake News stories that were released about my case. Furthermore I had to gain the best result possible which shows that I did not fight seven years for nothing. I've made 20 or more court appearances in which I represented myself before several judges who were not all nice and honorable. I've been to Luzerne County prison at least 10 times or more.

Although I know that it is next to impossible to commit disorderly conduct inside of a prison solitary confinement cell, it is not likely that this conviction holds any substance in the greater scheme of things.

The agreement between the parties to enter into a silent agreement that the only evidence to be considered was whether or not I was guilty of misconduct gave the other side the opportunity to save face.

"Likewise, to paraphrase Chinese master strategist Tu Mu "Show him a way to safely withdraw from the battle by creating in his mind an alternative to losing." Thus, when trying to bring a person into agreement with you, always leave him a face saving way out of a disagreement, a way of honorably abandoning his position".-Dr. Haha Lung, Ultimate Mind Control: Asian Arts of Mental Domination.

Both sides, I and the prosecutor had something to gain from this exchange. The prosecution got the appearance of justice for the alleged victims which in turn protects their public persona. I in turn gained the opportunity of an implicit acquittal on the Riot charges and other outrageous charges of throwing shit on officers.

If my actions of tying up the cell door amounted to disorderly conduct. I can deal with that, so be it. However the greater offenses which not only had the effect of dirtying my clothes but also my reputation were squashed. It was more than necessary to clear my name of said charges.

In fact the bench trial went so fast that even the Sheriffs were confused as to what had just occurred. After the hearing transpired, the sheriffs asked me, "was it over now?" I explained to them what had just took place. I don't think some of them liked the fact that in their minds I was wrongfully escaping felony charges of assault and Riot. That's why they kicked my supporters out of the hallway and prevented them from taking pictures.

Maybe the newspapers were confused too, however it was impossible to reach the conclusion that Keys was found guilty of throwing "shit' at guards as was stated in the newspapers. Such conclusion could not be gleaned from disorderly conduct charges. The conclusion of the local media was nothing more than classical spin to help the prosecutor appear to have proven his case against me, while the opposite were true. Meanwhile it's as clear as day that a misdemeanor disorderly conduct charge is a far cry from "Assault" of six "American hero" prison guards.

"By directing the first prong of attack into our foes minds we might eliminate the need to follow through with an actual physical attack". Dr. Haha Lung Cao Dai Kung Fu.

Throughout these seven years there were always doubters, fear mongers and spineless individuals telling me not to fight. At one point I considered taking a plea to "no time" for a misdemeanor simple assault, however for one reason or another, this did not take place. I am happy that this did not occur, because it would have given some credibility to the network of liars and their lies. Parole may have been an option at that point, however; it would be a privilege granted at the mercy of my captors, and grace and mercy is not their cup of tea.

"We become flexible, adaptive and versatile- adept at improvisation and innovation-- if for no other reason than because we had to in order to survive." -J. Paul Getty

Another factor that ran through my mind during the course of these seven years, was the fact that Northeast Pennsylvania is a hub for White Supremacist groups, Conservatives and blind American loyalists. This is a county where the voters still support the same District Attorneys who were complicit in the "Kids for Cash scheme". My logic for doubting that I could receive a fair jury in Luzerne County Pennsylvania had nothing to do with defeatism as stated by one of my co-defendants in Vice Magazine. Instead it had everything to do with mathematical calculations of weighing the pros and cons of an area known for corruption and racism.

For example 70% of Luzerne County voted for Donald trump. If majority of Luzerne County voted for that idiot who has been caught in 1000 lies, what would make me believe they would vote not guilty for me? Furthermore, the whole theory of delaying court dates as a chess strategy goes against classical war strategy. See Getty's five (numbers four and five): Billionaire Paul J. Getty (1892-1976) who made it his business to read men, pointed out five personality types of men when faced with obstacles:

1. The Helpless
2. Cowards
3. Flailers
4. Hole Pluggers and
5. True leaders

Getty said of Hole Pluggers:

"Defensive fighters who solve problems as they arise, whereas they may respond correctly and even effectively in the long run, they're always playing catch up because they respond only after a problem has fully manifested" (note; this runs contrary to the advice of Sun Tzu, Tao Te Ching, Machiavelli, and any other strategist worth their salt, all of whom knew how to deal with small problems-small enemies-before they become big problems-big enemies).

After being emergency transferred from Dallas to Frackville on the date of the alleged riot, I was denied breakfast and lunch by a Frackville prison guard, who told me that he would not let me get away with assaulting seven guards. I had no idea what the hell they were talking about, because at this particular time I had yet to receive any misconduct reports for the fake assaults. I said: "What the fuck are you talking about I assaulted seven guards". This lie would be repeated overtly and covertly at every institution that I went to, which caused officers to blindly strike out at me.

Over the years the false allegations continued to follow and most of the prison guards whom happen to be brain dead robots were not bright enough to realize that it's next to impossible to throw feces on seven guards from inside of a cell that has a sliding door. In other words unless I could reach my arm outside the door, the only angle that I could've throw something from is in a forward motion. (If I would have reached my hand outside of the door then I'm risking getting my arm crushed by a steel door). I've made some mistakes in my life, but I'm not that much of an idiot to have faith in the same prison guards who threatened to harm me. I knew they would have crushed my arm inside the door, if I reached out to throw something. Secondly the cameras on both sides of the cell block would have recorded this.

I recognized that in 2017 after a divided election with much division, along with strong racial and national issues in our country, this is not the time to have a jury trial for a politically and racially charged ordeal such as the Dallas 6 case. The small problems and small enemies who could have been dealt with and crushed years ago, now would have an even greater chance of achieving their wicked goals of additional prison time and a felony conviction. By attending a bench trial where the outcome was predetermined to be favorable, I avoided the unpredictability of a bias jury pool.

Paul J. Getty said of true leaders: "True leaders on the other hand, deal with little problems before they become big problems-big enemies. Attacked, true leaders decisively and effectively counter-attack. They know that "the best defense is a good offense".

I can now move on with my life and tell my own stories. F*@! the "Alternative Facts", ego-maniac philosophies and rhetorical bull-shit. If you want the truth of what it was like being transferred around the state for seven years between seven different prisons, attacked constantly for false charges of throwing shit on guards, you can get the truth directly from the man's (not the horses) mouth.

The cameras did not support their story. However the lack of video evidence did not stop some idiots from buying into their story. Obviously the state does not need video evidence to get juries to believe them. In reality we should have all been found "Not guilty" at the first trial. However somehow they must have convinced some of the jurors that a prisoner who covers a cell door is guilty of "riot", and that it was possible to strike a camera man in the back of the head, while the camera man was facing towards the cell filming the cell extraction.

Do you understand how big of an Air-head that someone has to be in order to believe in something so ridiculous as that? Well guess what? Welcome to Luzerne County, Pennsylvania, the home of Rush Limbaugh where nonsensical propaganda is at an all-time high, racism and White Nationalism has a major strong hold there in Northeastern Pennsylvania.

It's a miracle that most of the Dallas 6 did not receive any additional prison time or felony convictions, because we stuck to our guns. They tell you that America is the land of the free with liberty and justice for all. Well I'm here to tell you otherwise, and if you believe that America is the land of the free with liberty and justice for all, than you're one naive Mother*@*#@v1. Freedom is not free it must be fought for. I'm here to tell you that justice does not come from a blind lady with a sword. If you trust a blind person with a sword to give you your fair slice of justice, than you might as well go ahead and put your head on a guillotine and ask your worse enemy to chop it off, because you're a nincompoop.

In order to get justice we have to remove the blindfolds. America has been blinded by the Shenanigans of the politically astute mind-slayers. Once you remove the blind-folds from off the eyes of naive American jurors, then maybe you can receive justice. Justice comes with a price just like freedom. It's just for those who can afford it or for those who fight, but it sure isn't free.

"Few of us have cojones (nuts) big enough to challenge the status quo, to step "outside the box". Thus any time some rebel or malcontent does trespass social norms by challenging procedure and protocol, by questioning what it means to be a man or where a woman's place really is, those depending on such fickle social glue to hold their fragile world together are knocked out of the box. The amount of freedom in any society is directly proportionate to how many farts and "Fuck you's" you hear". Mind Control (Methods of Mayhem) Dr. Haha Lung.

Chapter 18
MEANINGFUL QUOTES FROM DALLAS 6

I sat here the past couple of days and thought and played out different scenarios in my head and the answer ends the same---STAND UP BEFORE THEY KILL Y OU
--Anthony Kelly

I'm one of the individuals that was shocked and tasered as well as shackled, handcuffed at the waist with pepper spray over my body. I was extracted in cell 47 and placed in cell 49... No toilet paper or working toilet or sink.
--Anthony Locke

The cell extraction team "came with violence and drew my blood splitting my head open over my eye whereas I had to get three stitches. Not to even mention how they bruised and injured the left side of my face and my right knee yeah they threw me in the hard cell naked with nothing but a tight restraint belt, barely allowing me to breathe correctly, my blood could not even circulate properly because of the tight handcuffs and shackles. I had no running water not even a piece of toilet paper, all I had was a hard cold frame, whereas I was going through convulsions all night because of the freezing cold I was without clothes in restraints over 24 hours. Around dinner the next day after the cell extraction I was transferred to SC Mahanoy. Mahanoy had me in a hard cell for a week until I saw PRC (Program Review Committee)
--Derrick Stanley

"So when we act like men and draw the line before tyranny, pledging our own lives, I think that bold and brave line of comradery and defiance should be respected and appreciated by everyone on both sides, because what we do here has and will continue to have long, reaching effects in the long run. I know I am a part of history and I will direct my script and the part I play in it. These men that I am proud to stand with deserve the utmost respect from all involved along with bonaf5ide support, anything short of that is a disservice and disrespect to this struggle.
--Duane Peters-El

Chapter 19
THE IMPORTANCE OF FIGHTING THIS CASE

It was important that we fight this case to send the message of inspiration to other people who may be falsely accused. It's far too many people who have been pressured by the system to plead guilty to false allegations, due to the fear of the consequences of what may occur if found guilty by a jury.

Secondly it was important to stand up for all prisoners in solitary confinement, all people of color and oppressed people who have been singled out by tyrants in the government. In the beginning, we were all charged with riot, in the end there was only one Dallas 6 member found guilty of riot, that is the one who plead guilty.

Four of the Dallas 6 came out unaffected by any punishment imposed by the state as the result of misdemeanor convictions and two were exonerated. I was charged with riot and six counts of felony aggravated harassment. In the end, I came out with a disorderly conduct conviction. That is the result of standing up for myself, and the support from my mother and all the other people that she rallied together for justice. Carrington Keys, the last of the Dallas 6 to stand trial. It may not be everything that I wanted but hey this is the price that men pay for standing up to an injustice system.

ALL POWER TO THE PEOPLE!

Chapter 20
WHY SOLITARY CONFINEMENT IS INHUMANE

From my more than 10 years' experience of solitary confinement, I witnessed the backlash of psychological injuries to many men including myself. The psychological effects of solitary confinement differ among each individual. Some of the people who are subject to solitary confinement begin to mentally deteriorate within days and others lose themselves over an extended period of time. Some of the Psychological effects include; lack of control over mental and verbal reactions, hyperactivity from lack of external stimulation, antisocial behavior, short term memory loss, shortened attention span, being lost in thought, daydreaming extensively and attention seeking behavior that is both abnormal and psychotic. Such behavior includes kicking on doors, banging on walls and sinks, screams in the middle of the night, paranoia and loss of sleep from 24 hour lights and the constant noise of the environment. Other behavior includes suicidal tendencies and violent reactions to the slightest gesture.

It also doesn't help that majority of the prisons are located in rural white America. Inside 8 state prisons and 3 county jails that I served time in, the most racist guards are given charge of feeding, showering and exercising black and Latino prisoners. This is an environment ripe for mistreatment and breeding ground for every injustice imaginable. This is certainly true for camp hill, Frackville, Mahanoy, Dallas and SCI retreat. Inmates in solitary confinement are sometimes treated so bad, that we are forced to take all necessary means to counter the mistreatment. Writing a letter to any branch of government is just not reasonable alternative, when a prisoner has not eaten in weeks. When guards control your entire existence including mail delivery. This may sound extreme or exaggerated to some, but after spending over 10 years in solitary confinement, I dare anyone to come forward and call me a liar.

What's the Solution?

By all means necessary it must end. We must educate the families of prisoners to become involved in the political process for the passing of new legislation and in putting people in office who will represent the issues of

the poor and disadvantaged segments of society. Solitary confinement as a form of physical and psychological torture is only one issue amidst many horrific crimes committed by the United States of America.
(Government=WE the People or them the people)

CONTACT AUTHOR

Write:
Carrington Keys EF4010
SCI Forest
Po Box 945
Marienville, PA 16239

Email:
connectnetwork.com (You have to subscribe and pay fee of at least $1)
Carrington Keys EF4010

Or

CONTACT COORDINATOR - JUSTICE FOR DALLAS 6

Shandre Delaney (mother of Carrington Keys)
Email: sd4hrc@gmail.com
Phn: 724-960-8284

Write:
Freedom46/HRC
PO Box 8561
Pittsburgh, PA 15220

ONLINE:
Blog - http://scidallas6.blogspot.com/
Facebook - http://tinyurl.com/justice4ck
Twitter Hashtags - #Dallas6   #Justice4Dallas6

Videos:
The Price Men Pay: Falsely Accused for Standing up for Justice -
http://tinyurl.com/ck-utube

"Why Solitary Confinement is Torture" by Molly Crabapple which features
Dallas 6 - http://tinyurl.com/dallas6solitary